HAIKUS

BY

PRINCETONIANS V

2021–2022

EDITED BY MAYUMI ITOH

(This is one of the 1,049 screen paintings of the Main
Palace of Nagoya Castle, which survived World War II.
Nagoya Castle was built in 1612 as a residence for
Tokugawa Yoshinao, the ninth son of Tokugawa Ieyasu,
the founder of the Tokugawa shogunate. In 1930, the castle
was designated as a National Treasure of Japan, but was
burnt down by the U.S. air raids on Nagoya in May 1945.
The 1,049 screen paintings had been evacuated to storage
and were saved. Their reproductions went on public
display at the newly restored Main Palace in 2018.)

In memoriam,

Earl Roy Miner

Contents

List of Photographs

All photographs in the text are credited below except for those that were taken by the editor.

Photograph 0. "Sunrise on the Wedded Rocks," taken by Tawashi2006, June 14, 2008, licensed by Creative Commons, https://commons.wikimedia.org/wiki/File:Sunrise_of_the_Wedded_Rocks.jpg.

Photograph 1. "Shiro zuisen (Paperwhite, *narcissus papyraceus*)," taken by Dominicus Johannes Bergsma, March 14, 2014, licensed by Creative Commons, https://commons. wikimedia.org/wiki/File:Narcissus_papyraceus_Paperwhite_02.JPG.

Photograph 2. "Seashell Collection," Cape Goza, Shima-chō, Shima, Mie prefecture, taken by the editor, August 18, 2012.

Photograph 3. "Dandelion Puffs," taken by the editor, May 4, 2019.

Photograph 10. "Bamboo Shoot," painting by Shimomura Kanzan (1873–1930), from Sankei Memorial Hall Collection, licensed by Wikimedia Commons, https://commons. wikimedia.org/wiki/ File: Bamboo_Shoot_by_Shimomura_Kanzan,_Sankei_Memori al_Hall.JPG.

Photograph 11. "Crabapple Blossoms in Winter," taken by the editor, November 18, 2019.

Photograph 12. "Red Fox," taken by the editor, June 23, 2020.

Notes on the Text

This is the fifth bilingual haiku anthology written by students and alumni of Princeton University, consisting of 108 original haikus in total.

This work categorized them according to the twelve months and the four seasons (plus the "new year" which constitutes an independent 'season' because of its importance to Japanese culture). This book presents each haiku in both Japanese and English so that non-Japanese-speaking readers fully appreciate them. The text is formatted in a way that the first page for a given haiku (on the left side) shows the original haiku in Japanese, which is made up of a combination of Chinese characters (*kanji*) and Japanese phonetic characters (*hiragana* and *katakana*).

Then, in order to facilitate a better understanding, especially for those who are studying Japanese, the original haiku is shown in a modern spelling only in *hiragana* and *katakana*. This allows readers to see how the haiku is exactly pronounced phonetically. There are many ways to pronounce specific *kanji* words, and the original Japanese haiku does not indicate how each *kanji* character is actually pronounced. Afterward, the identification of the season word—an essential element in haiku—for the haiku is given and some explanations of the cultural and historical backgrounds are added where applicable.

On the second page for a given haiku (on the right side), a romanization of the original Japanese haiku is provided, first, so that English-speaking readers can understand how the haiku is pronounced. The words in Roman letters are divided into smaller groups of syllables, for easier reading. Then, an English translation of the haiku is presented. Due to the structural differences between English and Japanese, the word order of the haiku in English might be different from that of the original haiku in Japanese. It is followed by the English translations of the season word and the explanations of the cultural and

historical backgrounds where applicable. This completes

the presentation of a given haiku.

For romanizing Japanese words, the Hepburn style

is primarily used, with macrons. However, macrons are not

used for words known in English without macrons, as for

Kyoto and Tokyo. Also, "n" is not converted to "m" for

words where it precedes "b, m, and p." Examples include

tonbo (dragonfly), instead of tombo; sanma (Pacific saury),

instead of samma; and tanpopo (dandelion), instead of

tampopo.

Acknowledgments

In publishing the fifth haiku anthology written by students
and alumni of Princeton University, I would like to express
my sincere appreciation to Anna Shields, Professor and
Chair of the Department of East Asian Studies, who has
supported this haiku writing group for several years. I
would also like to thank Martin Kern, Professor and former
Chair of the Department, Brian Steininger, Associate
Professor of the Department, Shinji Sato, Japanese
Language Program Director and Senior Lecturer of the
Department, and other Japanese Language Program
Lecturers—Tomoko Shibata, Hisae Matsui, Keiko Ono,
Yukari Tokumasu, Megumi Watanabe—and Jeff Heller,
Department Data and Project Coordinator, as well as all the
other faculty members and administrative assistants of the
Department, and Dr. Martin Heijdra, East Asian Library
and the Gest Collection Director, for their generous support
of this haiku seminar.

In addition to the regular fall and spring terms of the university's academic year, this group also met regularly for three months during the summer, so that students kept honing their haiku writing skills. They wrote poignant haikus, reflecting their life coping with the unprecedented Covid-19 pandemic for more than two years. Given that we cannot publish this anthology unless we submit the name of the editor as the copyright holder, I have put my name as such. This does not affect the fact that each haiku belongs to the student who actually wrote it.

*   *   *

This anthology is a memorial tribute to Earl Roy Miner (1927–2004), who was Professor of Japanese Literature at Princeton University, specializing in Japanese poetry. As an authority on English and Comparative Literature, he also served as president of the Milton Society of America, the American Society for 18th Century Studies, and the International Comparative Literature Association.

Notable pioneering works about Japanese poetry by Professor Miner include *The Japanese Tradition in British and American Literature* (Princeton University Press, 1958), *An Introduction to Japanese Court Poetry*, with Robert H. Brower (Stanford University Press, 1968), *Japanese Poetic Diaries* (University of California Press, 1969), and *Japanese Linked Poetry: An Account with Translations of Renga and Haikai Sequences* (Princeton University Press, 1979).

The study of Japanese poetry has flourished at Princeton University under the tutelage of Professor Miner, who contributed articles about haiku and renga in the definitive *The Princeton Encyclopedia of Poetry and Poetics*. His mission in promoting Japanese poetry has been carried on by the faculty and students of the Department of East Asian Studies and will be further enhanced by current and future faculty and students.

初寅や

　　家康公の

　　　　鞍馬行

2022 年は、寅年。季語の初寅（はつとら、鞍馬詣、くらまもうで）は、
新年最初の寅の日に毘沙門天を祀る鞍馬寺（京都市）に参詣する
こと。徳川家康（1543 年–1616 年）は、寅年生まれ。

Hatsu tora ya

　　Ieyasu kō no

　　　　Kurama yuki

The First Day of the Tiger

　　Lord Ieyasu is visiting

　　　　Kurama Temple

The year 2022 is The Year of the Tiger. Tokugawa Ieyasu
(1543–1616), the founder of the Tokugawa shogunate, was born
in the Year of the Tiger. It was a custom to visit Kurama
Temple on the first Day of the Tiger in the new year. In East
Asia, there is a twelve-day cycle, corresponding to the same 12
animals of the 12-year zodiac cycle.

Mayumi Itoh

New Year

Photograph 0. "Sunrise on the Wedded Rocks," taken by Tawashi2006, June 14, 2008, licensed by Creative Commons, https://commons.wikimedia.org/wiki/ File:Sunrise_of_the_Wedded_Rocks.jpg.

新光や

　　朝を迎えて

　　　　初日の出

しんこうや

　　あさをむかえて

　　　　はつひので

季語　初日の出（はつひので、新年を表す）

マイルズ・ハーン

Shinkō ya

    asa o mukae te

        hatsu hinode

The new light

    greets the dawn

        at the first sunrise

Season's word: hatsu hinode (first sunrise of the year; signifies new year)

Mylz Hahn

踏み出すか

　初日の照らす

　　第一歩

ふみだすか

　はつひのてらす

　　だいいっぽ

季語　初日（はつひ、新年）

メメット・ツナ・ウイサル

Fumi dasu ka

    hatsu hi no terasu

        dai ippo

The sun shines

    on my first step

        on New Year's Day

Season's word: hatsu hi (first sun on New Year's Day;

new year)

Mehmet Tuna Uysal

初霞

　　車窓に微笑む

　　　　君の顔

はつがすみ

　　しゃそうにほほえむ

　　　　きみのかお

季語　初霞（はつがすみ、新年）

李一一（リー・イーイー、リリー）

Hatsu gasumi

shasō ni hohoemu

kimi no kao

The first haze of the year

the smile on your face

reflecting on the car window

Season word: hatsu gasumi (first haze of the year; new year)

Li Yiyi (Lily)

重箱に

　　たくさんの色

　　　　お節かな

じゅうばこに

　　たくさんのいろ

　　　　おせちかな

季語　お節（おせち、新年）

「お節」は、お節料理のこと。

マイルズ・ハーン

Jūbako ni

takusan no iro

o sechi kana

The lacquered food box

the many colors

of the New Year's Day dishes

Season word: o sechi (New Year's Day dishes; new year)

Mylz Hahn

初夢や

　　翼広げて

　　　　大鳳の啼く

はつゆめや

　　つばさひろげて

　　　　おおとりのなく

季語　　初夢（はつゆめ、新年）

「大鳳」は、鳳凰のこと。

劉凱琳（エデリン・ラウ）

Hatsu yume ya

    tsubasa hiroge te

        Ōtori no naku

The first dream of the year

    the mystic Peng spreads its wings

        and lets out a cry

Season word: hatsu yume (first dream on the night of New Year's Day; new year)

Peng refers to the Phoenix.

Edelyn H. Lau

アラームの

　　始める二日

　　　　朝七時

アラームの

　　はじめるふつか

　　　　あさしちじ

季語　二日（ふつか、新年）

「二日」は、正月二日（1 月 2 日）のこと。正月二日は仕事始めの吉日。

メメット・ツナ・ウイサル

Alāmu no

hajimeru Futsuka

asa shichi ji

The Second Day of the new year

begins at 7 o'clock

with the sound of the alarm

Season's word: Futsuka (January 2; new year)

January 2 marks the beginning of the activities of the year.

Mehmet Tuna Uysal

清い朝

　　歌会始

　　　　皆座る

きよいあさ

　　うたかいはじめ

　　　　みなすわる

季語　歌会始（うたかいはじめ、新年）

マイルズ・ハーン

Kiyoi asa

    utakai hajime

        mina suwaru

The serene morning

    the first poetry reading

        everyone is sitting

Season's word: utakai hajime (first poetry reading of the

year; new year)

Mylz Hahn

January

Photograph 1. "Shiro zuisen (Paperwhite, *narcissus papyraceus*)," taken by Dominicus Johannes Bergsma, March 14, 2014, licensed by Creative Commons, https://commons. wikimedia.org/wiki/File:Narcissus_ papyraceus_Paperwhite_02.JPG.

風花や

　　ふわりと歌う

　　　　希望の詩

かざはなや

　　ふわりとうたう

　　　　きぼうのし

季語　風花（かざはな、晩冬）

「風花」は、晴天に、雪が風に舞うようにちらちらと降ること
をさす。

劉凱琳（エデリン・ラウ）

Kaza hana ya

    fuwaru to utau

        kibō no shi

The snowflakes

    rush not

        and hum a verse of hope

Season word: kaza hana *(lit.,* 'wind flower' refers to

snowflakes; late winter)

Edelyn H. Lau

波の花

　　岩にぶつかり

　　　　花と散る

なみのはな

　　いわにぶつかり

　　　　はなとちる

季語　波の花（なみのはな、晩冬）

マイルズ・ハーン

Nami no hana

    iwa ni butsukari

        hana to chiru

The winter sea waves

    crash against the rocks

        and disappear like flower petals

Season word: nami no hana (winter sea waves that look

like flower petals; late winter)

Mylz Hahn

日当たりや

　　干し大根と

　　　　祖母の手と

ひあたりや

　　ほしだいこんと

　　　　そぼのてと

季語　干し大根（ほしだいこん、三冬）

劉小雨（リュウ・シャオユー）

Hiatari ya

    hoshi daikon to

        sobo no te to

The sun shines

    upon the dried giant radish

        and grandmother's dry hand

Season word: hoshi daikon (dried giant radish; all winter)

Liu Xiaoyu

聞こえるか

　　しぶきを上げる

　　　　潮花よ

きこえるか

　　しぶきをあげる

　　　　しおばなよ

季語　潮花（しおばな、晩冬）

メメット・ツナ・ウイサル

Kikoeru ka

    shibuki o ageru

        shio bana yo

Do you hear

    the great splashing

        of the winter sea wave blossoms

Season word: shio bana (winter sea waves that look like

flowers; late winter)

Mehmet Tuna Uysal

いつの間に

　　凍てついていた

　　　　恋心

いつのまに

　　いてついていた

　　　　こいごころ

季語　凍てつく（凍てる、いてる、三冬）

王志茜（山口茜）

Itsuno ma ni

   ite tsuite ita

      koi gokoro

How had I not noticed

   —known this—

      that my heart had frozen over

Season word: ite tsuku (iteru, to freeze; all winter)

Akaneh Wang

先見えぬ

　　時の節東風

　　　「春よ来い」

さきみえぬ

　　ときのせちごち

　　　「はるよこい」

季語　　節東風（せちごち、晩冬）

「節東風」は、瀬戸内あたりで、陰暦の十二月頃吹く東より
の風をいう。春の訪れが近いことを知らせる風である。

李一一（リー・イーイー、リリー）

Saki mienu

toki no sechi gochi

"Haru yo koi"

The east wind

in the unpredictable future

the whisper of "May Spring Come"

Season word: sechi gochi (east wind blowing during the

new year season, in the old calendar; late winter)

Li Yiyi (Lily)

雪片や

　　落ち葉のように

　　　　地を覆う

せっぺんや

　　おちばのように

　　　　ちをおおう

季語　雪片（せっぺん、晩冬）

マイルズ・ハーン

Seppen ya

    ochiba no yō ni

        chi o ōu

Snowflakes

    blanket the earth

        like fallen leaves

Season word: seppen (snowflakes; late winter)

Mylz Hahn

水仙や

　　真っ白の世に

　　　　凛と咲く

すいせんや

　　まっしろのよに

　　　　りんとさく

季語　　水仙（すいせん、晩冬）

この句の水仙は、白水仙をさす。

劉凱琳（エデリン・ラウ）

Suisen ya

    masshiro no yo ni

        rin to saku

Narcissus

    bloom valiantly

        in a pure white world

Season word: suisen (shiro zuisen, **paperwhite**, *narcissus papyraceus*; late winter)

Narcissus are white flowers that signify late winter while daffodils are yellow flowers that signify mid-spring.

Edelyn H. Lau

February

Photograph 2. "Seashell Collection," Cape Goza, Shima-chō, Shima, Mie prefecture, taken by the editor, August 18, 2012.

薄氷や

　　　木を包み込み

　　　　枝震う

うすらいや

　　　きをつつみこみ

　　　　えだふるう

季語　薄氷（うすらい、初春）

マイルズ・ハーン

Usurai ya

   ki o tsutsumi komi

      eda furū

The thin ice

   engulfs the tree

      shivering branches

Season word: usurai (thin ice; early spring)

Mylz Hahn

故郷の

　　微風に揺れる

　　　　猫柳

ふるさとの

　　びふうにゆれる

　　　　ねこやなぎ

季語　猫柳（ねこやなぎ、初春）

劉凱琳（エデリン・ラウ）

Furusato no

    bifū ni yureru

        neko yanagi

In my hometown

    pussy willows sway

        in a gentle breeze

Season word: neko yanagi (pussy willow; early spring)

Edelyn H. Lau

山焼きや

　　夜空を燃やせ

　　　竜の息

やまやきや

　　よぞらをもやせ

　　　りゅうのいき

季語　　山焼き（やまやき、初春）

「山焼き」は、牛馬の飼料の草や山菜類の発育を促し、害
虫を駆除するために、村里に近い野山を焼くこと。

ミーナ・ケセン

Yama yaki ya

yozora o moyase

ryū no iki

Burning the mountain

Make the night glow red

like a dragon's breath

Season words: yama yaki (a practice of burning mountains

to rejuvenate the field and farm; early spring)

Mina Quesen

笑い声

　　ほんのり香る

　　　　春蜜柑

わらいごえ

　　ほんのりかおる

　　　　はるみかん

季語　春蜜柑（はるみかん、三春）

王志茜（山口茜）

Warai goe

hon'nori kaoru

haru mikan

The sound of laughter

the spring breeze carries

along the scent of sweet citrus

Season word: haru mikan (species of mikan harvested in

spring such as Iyokan; all spring)

Akaneh Wang

今週に

　　低温が来る

　　　　春寒し

こんしゅうに

　　ていおんがくる

　　　　はるさむし

季語　春寒（はるさむ、初春）

マイルズ・ハーン

Koshū ni

    teion ga kuru

        haru samushi

This week

    low temperatures are expected

        spring chill

Season word: haru samu (cold spell in spring; early spring)

Mylz Hahn

光る風

　　運ぶ七色

　　　　花畑

ひかるかぜ

　　はこぶなないろ

　　　　はなばたけ

季語　光る風（風光る、かぜひかる、三春）

メメット・ツナ・ウイサル

Hikaru kaze

    hakobu nana iro

        hana batake

The wind shines

    carrying the seven colors

        to the flower field

Season word: hikaru kaze (kaze hikaru, wind shines; all

spring)

Mehmet Tuna Uysal

窓越しに

　　西日をよぎる

　　　　夕雲雀

まどごしに

　　にしびをよぎる

　　　　ゆうひばり

季語　夕雲雀（ゆうひばり、三春）

劉凱琳（エデリン・ラウ）

Mado goshi ni

    nishi bi o yogiru

        yū hibari

Through the window

    an evening lark

        passing by the setting sun

Season word: yū hibari (evening lark; all spring)

Edelyn H. Lau

桜貝

　　手のひらに睡る

　　　宝物

さくらがい

　　てのひらにねる

　　　たからもの

季語　桜貝（さくらがい、三春）

王志茜（山口茜）

Sakura gai

te no hira ni noru

takara mono

A delicate pink shell

nestled in a child's hand

a timeless treasure

Season word: sakura gai (pink seashell; all spring)

Akaneh Wang

如月や

　　　授業と花は

　　　　　新しく

きさらぎや

　　　じゅぎょうとはなは

　　　　　あたらしく

季語　如月（きさらぎ、仲春）

「如月」は、旧暦二月の異称。

マイルズ・ハーン

Kisaragi ya

jugyō to hana wa

atarashiku

February

classes and flowers

both have a new start

Season word: Kisaragi (February in the old calendar; mid-spring)

Mylz Hahn

March

Photograph 3. "Dandelion Puffs," taken by the editor, May 4, 2019.

柔らかな

　　光の笑顔

　　　　雪解けよ

やわらかな

　　ひかりのえがお

　　　　ゆきどけよ

季語　　雪解け（ゆきどけ、仲春）

メメット・ツナ・ウイサル

Yawaraka na

   hikari no egao

      yuki doke yo

Gently

   the smile of the sun

      melts the snow

Season word: yuki doke (melting snow; mid-spring)

Mehmet Tuna Uysal

雪解や

　　空からの水

　　　　地に戻る

ゆきどけや

　　そらからのみず

　　　　ちにもどる

季語　雪解け（ゆきどけ、仲春）

マイルズ・ハーン

Yuki doke ya

    sora kara no mizu

        chi ni modoru

Melting snow

    the water from the sky

        returns to the earth

Season word: yuki doke (melting snow; mid-spring)

Mylz Hahn

朝寝坊

　　啓蟄の日に

　　　　笑う虫

あさねぼう

　　けいちつのひに

　　　　わらうむし

季語　啓蟄(けいちつ、仲春)

「啓蟄」は、二十四節気の一つで、通常 3 月 6 日頃に始ま

り、その日及び、その日から 2 週間の期間をさす。

ルーカス・スチュワート

Asa nebō

Keichitsu no hi ni

warau mushi

The morning I sleep in

the Day of Insects Crawling Out

a bug smiles

Season word: Keichitsu (the Day of Insects Crawling Out;

mid-spring)

Keichitsu refers to one of the Twenty-four small seasons,

which begins around March 6, depending on the year, and

lasts for two weeks.

Lucas Stewart

蒲公英や

　　風に散るのは

　　　　誰の涙か

たんぽぽや

　　かぜにちるのは

　　　　だれのなみだか

季語　蒲公英（たんぽぽ、仲春）

劉凱琳（エデリン・ラウ）

Tanpopo ya

    kaze ni chiru nowa

        dare no namida ka

Oh, dandelions

    whose tear are scattering

      in the wind

Season word: tanpopo (dandelion; mid-spring)

Edelyn H. Lau

軍艦に

　　沈む夕日の

　　　　彼岸かな

ぐんかんに

　　しずむゆうひの

　　　　ひがんかな

季語　彼岸（ひがん、**仲春**）

李一一（リー・イーイー、リリー）

Gunkan ni

shizumu yūhi no

Higan kana

Behind the battleship

sinks the sun

on the spring equinox

Season word: Higan (vernal equinox; mid-spring)

Li Yiyi (Lily)

鳥帰る

　　次会う時に

　　　　伝えよう

とりかえる

　　つぎあうときに

　　　　つたえよう

季語　鳥帰る（とりかえる、仲春）

「鳥帰る」は、雁、鴨、白鳥など、日本で越冬した渡り鳥が
北方のシベリアへ去ることをさす。

王恚茜（山口茜）

Tori kaeru

    tsugi au toki ni

        tsutaeyō

Birds returning to the north

    next time we meet

        I promise I'll tell you those words

Season word: tori kaeru (birds returning to the north; mid-spring)

Birds, such as geese and swans, winter in Japan and return to Siberia in the spring.

Akaneh Wang

春一番

　　　　君の歌声

　　　　　　鳴り響く

はるいちばん

　　　きみのうたごえ

　　　　　なりひびく

季語　春一番（はるいちばん、**仲春**）

「春一番」は、立春後から春分の間に初めて吹く南寄りの

突風のこと。

メメット・ツナ・ウイサル

Haru ichiban

kimi no uta goe

nari hibiku

The first spring gust

your song

echoes in it

Season word: haru ichiban (first spring gust; mid-spring)

Mehmet Tuna Uysal

早い朝

　　外が見えない

　　　　春霞

はやいあさ

　　そとがみえない

　　　　はるがすみ

季語　春霞（はるがすみ、三春）

マイルズ・ハーン

Hayai asa

soto ga mienai

haru gasumi

Early morning

I can't see outside

the day of spring haze

Season word: haru gasumi (spring haze; all spring)

Mylz Hahn

April

Photograph 4. "Fallen Cherry Blossom Carpet," taken by
the editor, May 10, 2013.

拭き落とす

　　車窓の花は

　　　　別れ霜

ふきおとす

　　しゃそうのはなは

　　　　わかれじも

季語　別れ霜（わかれじも、晩春）

李一一（リー・イーイー、リリー）

Fuki otosu

    shasō no hana wa

        wakare jimo

The flowers

    I wiped from the car windows

        the last frost of spring

Season word: wakare jimo (last frost of the season; late

spring)

Li Yiyi (Lily)

この香り

　　桜吹雪の

　　　　芳しき

このかおり

　　さくらふぶきの

　　　　かぐわしき

季語　桜吹雪（さくらふぶき、晩春）

マイルズ・ハーン

Kono kaori

    sakura fubuki no

        kaguwashiki

The scent

    of the cherry blossom shower

        splendid indeed

Season word: sakura fubuki (falling cherry blossom petals

like shower; late spring)

Mylz Hahn

戦ぐ草

　　震える鼠

　　　　夢見る子猫

そよぐくさ

　　ふるえるねずみ

　　　　ゆめみるこねこ

季語　子猫（こねこ、晩春）

ルーカス・スチュワート

Soyogu kusa

    furueru nezumi

        yume miru koneko

Swaying grass

    the trembling mouse

        so dreams the kitten

Season word: koneko (kitten; late spring)

Lucas Stewart

昼下がり

　　マンゴー開く

　　　　パパの手に

ひるさがり

　　マンゴーひらく

　　　　パパのてに

季語　マンゴーの花（マンゴーのはな、三春）

ミーナ・ケセン

Hiru sagari

   mangō hiraku

      papa no te ni

An afternoon

   the mango blooms

      in Papa's hands

Season word: mangō no hana (mango blooms; all spring)

Mina Quesen

草の中

　　　色々な色

　　　　　復活祭よ

くさのなか

　　　いろいろないろ

　　　　　ふっかつさいよ

季語　復活祭（ふっかつさい、晩春）

マイルズ・ハーン

Kusa no naka

   iro iro na iro

      Fukkatsu sai yo

In the grass

   many colors

      It's Easter

Season word: Fukkatsu sai (Easter; late spring)

Mylz Hahn

論文を

　　一つだけ読む

　　　　春の暮

ろんぶんを

　　ひとつだけよむ

　　　　はるのくれ

論文を

季語　春の暮（はるのくれ、三春）

李一一（リー・イーイー、リリー）

Ronbun o

   hitotsu dake yomu

      haru no kure

Reading

   only a single article

      in the spring evening

Season word: harr no kure (spring evening; all spring)

Li Yiyi (Lily)

春の丘

　　飛んできた鳥

　　　枝に降り

はるのおか

　　とんできたとり

　　　えだにおり

季語　春の丘（はるのおか、三春）

ルーカス・スチュワート

Haru no oka

    tonde kita tori

        eda ni ori

Atop a hill in the spring

    a bird descends from above

        and perches anew

Season word: haru no oka (hill in spring; all spring)

Lucas Stewart

糸柳

　　葉のカスケード

　　　枝を巻く

いとやなぎ

　　はのカスケード

　　　えだをまく

季語　糸柳（いとやなぎ、晩春）

マイルズ・ハーン

Ito yanagi

ha no casukēdo

eda o maku

A weeping willow

a cascade of leaves

shrouds the branches

Season word: ito yanagi (weeping willow; late spring)

Mylz Hahn

May

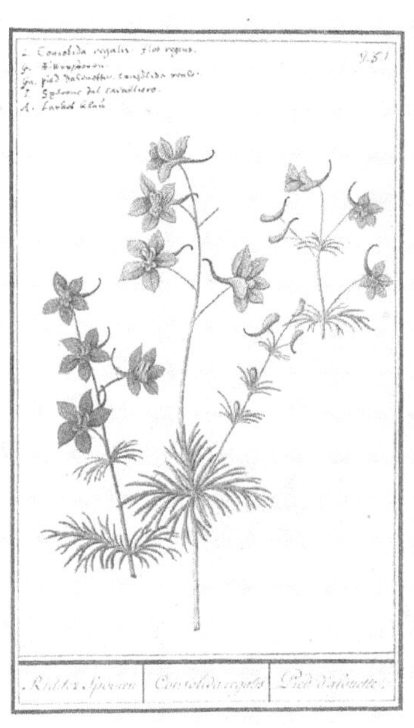

Photograph 5. "Delphinium," botanical illustration (between 1596 and 1610), Historia Naturalis van Rudolf II, licensed by Wikimedia Commons, https://commons. wikimedia.org/wiki/File:Ridderspoor_(Delphinium)_Ridde r_Spooren._Consolida_regalis._Pied_d'alouette_(titel_op_ object),_RP-T-BR-2017-1-10-55.jpg.

卯波打つ海岸

　　　驟雨打つ「潮騒」

うなみうつかいがん

　　　しゅううつ「しおさい」

季語　卯波（うなみ、初夏）　驟雨（しゅうう、三夏）

「卯波」は、陰暦四月、卯の花が咲く頃に海に立つ波のこと。俳句では、5月5日より夏となる。この句は、三島由紀夫の小説、『潮騒』（1954年）より連想。

李一一（リー・イーイー、リリー）

Unami utsu kaigan

shūu utsu "shiosai"

The early summer wave beats the coast

the shower beats "the sound of waves"

Season words: unami (early summer wave; early summer)

and shūu (summer shower; all summer)

This haiku is inspired by Mishima Yukio's novel, *Shiosai*

(*The Sound of Waves*, 1954).

Li Yiyi (Lily)

新茶摘む

　　娘の細い手の

　　　　残り香よ

しんちゃつむ

　　このほそいての

　　　　のこりかよ

季語　新茶摘む（しんちゃつむ、初夏）

劉凱琳（エデリン・ラウ）

Shin cha tsumu

ko no hosoi te no

nokori ka yo

Picking the first tea leaves of the season

the girl's slender hands

the lingering scent

Season word: shin cha tsumu (to harvest the first green tea
leaves of the season; early summer)

Edelyn H. Lau

黄揚羽よ

　　空中に舞う

　　　　初舞台

きあげはよ

　　くうちゅうにまう

　　　　はつぶたい

季語　黄揚羽（きあげは、三夏）

玉真有梨

Ki ageha yo

kūchū ni mau

hatsu butai

A swallowtail

dancing in the air

its debut on stage

Season word: **ki ageha** (swallowtail, a species of butterfly;

all summer)

Yuri Tamama

更衣

　　ふと思い出す

　　　　幼少期

ころもがえ

　　ふとおもいだす

　　　　ようしょうき

季語　更衣（ころもがえ、初夏）

「更衣」は、初夏に、冬の着物から夏の着物に替える習慣

のことをさす。

王志茜（山口茜）

Koromo gae

　　futo omoidasu

　　　　yōshō ki

Seasonal clothing change

　　fleeting thoughts of childhood

　　　　distant summer days

Season word: koromo gae (seasonal change into summer

clothing; early summer)

Akaneh Wang

カーディナル

　　夏の光に

　　　　金になる

カーディナル

　　なつのひかりに

　　　　きんになる

季語　夏の光（なつのひかり、三夏）

ミーナ・ケセン

Kādinaru

   natsu no hikari ni

      kin ni naru

The cardinal

   in the summer sun ray

      becomes gold

Season word: **natsu no hikari** (summer sunlight; all

summer)

Mina Quesen

花桐や

　　強く吹いたら

　　　　鳴るかしら

はなぎりや

　　つよくふいたら

　　　　なるかしら

季語　花桐（はなぎり、桐の花、初夏）

劉凱琳（エデリン・ラウ）

Hana giri ya

    tsuyoku fuitara

        naru kashira

The paulownia blossoms

    if blown strongly

        will they ring

Season word: hana giri (kiri no hana, paulownia, or

princess tree blossoms; early summer)

Edelyn H. Lau

夏の夕

　　心明るく

　　　　散歩する

なつのゆう

　　こころあかるく

　　　　さんぽする

季語　夏の夕（なつのゆう、三夏）

メメット・ツナ・ウイサル

Natsu no yū

kokoro akaruku

sanpo suru

Summer evening

strolling

with bright heart and light feet

Season word: natsu no yū (**summer evening**; all summer)

Mehmet Tuna Uysal

客の猫

　　夏の夕空

　　　　柑子色

きゃくのねこ

　　なつのゆうぞら

　　　　こうじいろ

季語　夏の夕空（なつのゆうぞら、三夏）

シャンタヌ・ラムジ

Kyaku no neko

    natsu no yū zora

        kōji iro

A visiting cat

    as orange as

        the summer evening sky

Season word: natsu no yū zora (summer evening sky;

all summer)

Shantanu Ramji

食卓に

　　残る夏柑

　　　　ほろ苦し

しょくたくに

　　のこるなつかん

　　　　ほろにがし

季語　夏柑（なつかん、夏蜜柑、なつみかん、初夏）

劉凱琳（エデリン・ラウ）

Shokutaku ni

nokoru natsu kan

horo nigashi

Left on the dining table

the Japanese summer orange

tastes bitter sweet

Season word: natsu kan (natsu mikan, Japanese summer

orange; early summer)

Edelyn H. Lau

June

Photograph 6. "Twin Rabbits," taken by the editor, June 19, 2020.

入梅や

　　朝の坂道

　　　　伸びて行く

にゅうばいや

　　あさのさかみち

　　　　のびていく

季語　入梅（にゅうばい、**仲夏**）

「入梅」は、梅雨入りのことをさす。

メメット・ツナ・ウイサル

Nyūbai ya

   asa no saka michi

      nobite yuku

The beginning of the rainy season

   the morning hike up the hill

      stretches ahead

Season word: nyūbai (beginning of the rainy season; mid-summer)

Mehmet Tuna Uysal

青嵐

　　悲しい寡婦の

　　　　白髪吹く

あおあらし

　　かなしいかふの

　　　　しらがふく

季語　　青嵐（あおあらし、三夏）

「青嵐」は、青葉の茂る頃に吹きわたる、やや強い風のこと
をさす。

劉凱琳（エデリン・ラウ）

Ao arashi

kanashii kafu no

shiraga fuku

The wind blowing through the fresh verdure

combs through

the widow's grey hair

Season word: ao arashi (fresh summer wind during the

time of lush green; all summer)

Edelyn H. Lau

壺の中

　　　小さな星よ

　　　　　蛍狩

つぼのなか

　　　小さなほしよ

　　　　　ほたるがり

季語　蛍狩（ほたるがり、仲夏）

マイルズ・ハーン

Tsubo no naka

    chiisana hoshi yo

        hotaru gari

Inside the vase

    are tiny stars

        firefly catching

Season word: hotaru gari (firefly catching; mid-summer)

Mylz Hahn

短夜は

　　なんでわざわざ

　　　　目閉じるの

みじかよは

　　なんでわざわざ

　　　　めとじるの

季語　短夜（みじかよ、三夏）

ナタリー・ディアス

Mijika yo wa

    nan de waza waza

        me tojiru no

The short summer nights

    why bother

        closing your eyes

Season word: **mijika yo (short summer night**; all summer)

Natalie Diaz

アイスティー

　　外出の味

　　　　懐かしい

アイスティー

　　　がいしゅつのあじ

　　　　なつかしい

季語　アイスティー（三夏）

この句は、コロナ禍の心境を詠む。

玉真有梨

Aisu tii

gaishutsu no aji

natsukashii

Cold iced tea

the sweet taste of going out

Oh, I missed it so

Season word: aisu tii (**iced tea**; all summer)

This haiku refers to frustration during Covid-19.

Yuri Tamama

飛燕草

　　猫と戯れ

　　　　尾の踊り

ひえんそう

　　ねことたわむれ

　　　　おのおどり

季語　飛燕草（ひえんそう、仲夏）

ミーナ・ケセン

Hiensō

    neko to tawamure

       o no odori

The delphinium

    plays with the cat

       the dance of tails

Season word: hiensō (delphinium; mid-summer)

Mina Quesen

銀世界

　　兎跳ね飛ぶ

　　　　夏の夢

ぎんせかい

　　うさぎはねとぶ

　　　　なつのゆめ

季語　　夏の夢（なつのゆめ、三夏）

兎は、通常、冬の季語（三冬）であるが、この句では、夏の
夢に登場するので、季語として使われていない。

ルーカス・スチュワート

Gin sekai

    usagi hane tobu

        natsu no yume

The field of silver snow

    the hare jumps around

        the summer dream

Season word: natsu no yume (**summer dread**; all summer)

Hare (rabbit) is a season word of winter, but this is not used

as such in this haiku, as it refers to a summer dream.

Lucas Stewart

蛍狩

　　闇に煌く

　　　　森の星

ほたるがり

　　やみにきらめく

　　　　もりのほし

季語　蛍狩（ほたるがり、仲夏）

メメット・ツナ・ウイサル

Hotaru gari

    yami ni kirameku

        mori no hoshi

Firefly catching

    twinkling in darkness

        the forest of stars

Season word: **hotaru gari** (**firefly catching**; mid-summer)

Mehmet Tuna Uysal

走馬灯

　　走り続ける

　　　　我が人生

そうまとう

　　はしりつづける

　　　　わがじんせい

季語　　走馬灯（そうまとう、廻り燈籠、三夏）

「走馬灯」は、影絵が回転しながら映るように細工された燈
籠のこと。

主志茜（山口茜）

Sōmatō

    hashiri tsuzukeru

        waga jinsei

The revolving lantern with shadow pictures

    we keep on running

        life is but a fleeting cycle of wonder

Season word: sōmatō (revolving lantern with shadow

pictures; all summer)

Akaneh Wang

July

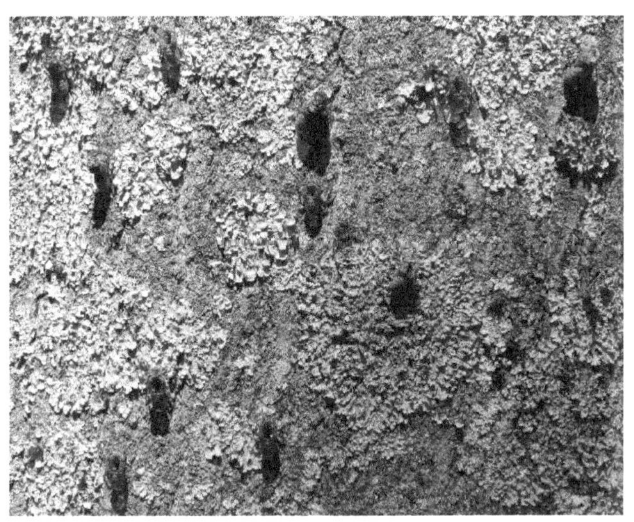

Photograph 7. "Cyclic Cicada Brood X," taken by the editor, May 21, 2021.

雲海を

　　超えて旅立つ

　　　　博士号

うんかいを

　　こえてたびだつ

　　　　はくしごう

季語　雲海（うんかい、晩夏）

李――（リー・イーイー、リリー）

Unkai o

koete tabi datsu

hakushi gō

Flying above the sea of clouds

I set off on my journey

for the Ph.D.

Season word: unkai (**sea of clouds**; late summer)

Li Yiyi (Lily)

睡蓮や

　　彼方の思い

　　　　連れて来る

すいれんや

　　かなたのおもい

　　　　つれてくる

季語　睡蓮（すいれん、晩夏）

この句は、クリスティーナ・ロセッティ（1830年–1894年）の

詩 "Ferry Me Across the Water" を引用する。

劉凱琳（エデリン・ラウ）

Suiren ya

    kanata no omoi

        tsurete kuru

Oh, water lilies

    ferry the distant warmth

        across the water

Season word: suiren (water lilies; late summer)

This is a reference to "Ferry Me Across the Water" by Christina Rossetti (s1830–1894).

Edelyn H. Lau

蝉の声

　　ただし今年は

　　　　ご勘弁

せみのこえ

　　ただしことしは

　　　　ごかんべん

季語　蝉（せみ、晩夏）

この句は、2021年に大量発生した周期蝉、ブルード
X（17年周期）を詠む。

玉真有梨

Semi no koe

tadashi kotoshi wa

go kanben

Cicadas chirping

soothing except this summer

too many outside

Season word: **semi no koe** (cicadas chirping; late summer)

This haiku refers to the cyclic cicada, Brood X, that emerged in 2021.

Yuri Tamama

雲海や

　　機上に見える

　　　　竜の床

うんかいや

　　きじょうにみえる

　　　　りゅうのとこ

季語　雲海（うんかい、晩夏）

ミーナ・ケセン

Unkai ya

kijō ni mieru

ryū no toko

Sea of cloud

the dragon's bed

seen from the airplane

Season word: unkai (**sea of clouds**; late summer)

Mina Quesen

朝曇り

　　天界の褄

　　　　見えぬ星

あさぐもり

　　てんかいのつま

　　　　みえぬほし

季語　朝曇り（あさぐもり、晩夏）

ルーカス・スチュワート

Asa gumori

    tenkai no tsuma

      mienu hoshi

Dawn's gray complexion

    In flowing skirt clad heaven

      Night's twinkle obscured

Season word: asa gumori (hazy morning; late summer)

Lucas Stewart

熱帯夜

　　寝てはならない

　　　　我が情火

ねったいや

　　ねてはならない

　　　　わがじょうか

季語　熱帯夜（ねったいや、**晩夏**）

この句は、ジャコモ・プッチーニ（1858 年—1924 年）の歌劇、トゥーランドット (*Turandot*) の "Nessun Dorma" を引用する。

劉凱琳（エデリン・ラウ）

Nettai ya

    netewa nara nai

      waga jōka

A torrid night

    let no one sleep

      my flame of love

Season word: nettai ya (*lit.*, 'tropical night' refers to hot

night; late summer)

This is a reference to "Nessun Dorma" from opera

Turandot by Giacomo Puccini (1858–1924).

Edelyn H. Lau

空蝉や

　　ザックザックと

　　　　踏む気持ち

うつせみや

　　ザックザックと

　　　　ふむきもち

季語　　空蝉（うつせみ、晩夏）

この句は、2021 年に大量発生した周期蝉、ブルード
X（17 年周期）を詠む。

ウディット・バス

Utsu semi ya

zakku zakku to

fumu kimochi

Crunch crunch

stepping on cicada's shells

I feel terrible

Season word: utsu semi (cicada's shell; late summer)

This haiku refers to the cyclic cicada, Brood X, that emerged in 2021.

Udit Basu

いつか見た

　　落ち葉の如き

　　　　夏の果

いつかみた

　　おちばのごとき

　　　　なつのはて

季語　夏の果（なつのはて、晩夏）

メメット・ツナ・ウイサル

Itsuka mita

   ochiba no gotoku

     natsu no hate

Summer ends

   like the fallen leaves

     I had seen in the past

Season word: natsu no hate (end of summer; late summer)

Mehmet Tuna Uysal

夏の末

　　高校生の

　　　　課題の仮面

なつのすえ

　　こうこうせいの

　　　　かだいのかめん

季語　夏の末（なつのすえ、晩夏）

ルーカス・スチュワート

Natsu no sue

kōkōsei no

kadai no kamen

Setting summer

What's ahead of students' heads:

That which school begets

Season word: natsu no sue (end of summer; late summer)

Lucas Stewart

August

Photograph 8. "Red Dragonfly (Ruddy Darter)," taken by Quartl, August 17, 2011, licensed by Wikimedia Commons, https://commons.wikimedia.org/wiki/File: Sympetrum_sanguineum_qtl13.jpg.

天の川

　　　身を投げる人

　　　　　長い列

あまのがわ

　　　みをなげるひと

　　　　　ながいれつ

季語　天の川（あまのがわ、初秋）

俳句では、8月7日から秋となる。

劉凱琳（エデリン・ラウ）

Ama no gawa

mi o nageru hito

nagai retsu

The Milky Way

a long line of travelers

waiting to throw themselves in

Season word: Ama no gawa (Milky Way; early autumn)

In haiku, August 7 marks the beginning of autumn.

Edelyn H. Lau

秋風や

　　一瞬に呼ぶ

　　　　友の顔

あきかぜや

　　いっしゅんによぶ

　　　　とものかお

季語　秋風（あきかぜ、三秋）

メメット・ツナ・ウイサル

Aki kaze ya

    isshun ni yobu

        tomo no kao

Autumn wind

    a friendly face is lit

        in a moment

Season word: aki kaze (autumn wind; all autumn)

Mehmet Tuna Uysal

流星や

　　暗闇の中

　　　　散ってゆく

りゅうせいや

　　くらやみのなか

　　　　ちってゆく

季語　流星（りゅうせい、三秋）

玉真有梨

Ryūsei ya

    kura yami no naka

        chitte yuku

Oh, the shooting star

    disappearing bit by bit

        in the dark unknown

Season's word: ryūsei (shooting star; all autumn)

Yuri Tamama

黒い空

　　　橙色の

　　　　　月の夜

くろいそら

　　　だいだいいろの

　　　　　つきのよる

季語　月の夜（つきのよる、三秋）

マイルズ・ハーン

Kuroi sora

daidai iro no

tsuki no yoru

The black sky

looks orange

in the moonlight

Season's word: tsuki no yoru (moonlit night; all autumn)

Mylz Hahn

蜻蛉去る

　　ページに残る

　　　　草の香よ

とんぼさる

　　ページにのこる

　　　　くさのかよ

季語　　蜻蛉（とんぼ、三秋）

李一一（リー・イーイー、リリー）

161

Tonbo saru

    pēji ni nokoru

        kusa no ka yo

The dragonfly flew away

    from the page of the book

        leaving a scent of the grass behind

Season word: tonbo (dragonfly; all autumn)

Li Yiyi (Lily)

流れ星

　　あの日願った

　　　　「好きでした」

ながれぼし

　　あのひねがった

　　　　「すきでした」

季語　流れ星（ながれぼし、三秋）

王志茜（山口茜）

Nagare boshi

ano hi negatta

"Suki deshita"

Shooting star goes past

once recalls my foolish wish

"I hope you like me too"

Season word: nagare boshi (shooting star; all autumn)

Akaneh Wang

天の川

　　　星を育てて

　　　　　夢を生む

あまのがわ

　　　ほしをそだてて

　　　　　ゆめをうむ

季語　天の川（あまのがわ、初秋）

ミーナ・ケセン

Ama no gawa

hoshi o sodate te

yume o umu

The Milky Way

nurses the stars

making dreams

Season word: Ama no gawa (Milky Way; early autumn)

Mina Quesen

秋の陽や

　　マスクの後ろ

　　　　涙あり

あきのひや

　　マスクのうしろ

　　　　なみだあり

季語　秋の陽（あきのひ、三秋）

ジェミーマ・ウィリアムズ

Aki no hi ya

    masuku no ushiro

        namida ari

The autumn sun

    behind its mask

        there are tears

Season word: aki no hi (autumn sun; all autumn)

This refers to the Covid-19 pandemic.

Jemima Williams

September

Photograph 9. "Cosmos," taken by the editor, August 13, 2021.

秋桜

　　涼しい朝に

　　　　咲く桜

あきざくら

　　すずしいあさに

　　　　さくさくら

季語　秋桜（あきざくら、コスモス、仲秋）

メメット・ツナ・ウイサル

Aki zakura

suzushii asa ni

saku sakura

The cosmos

the cherry blossoms of autumn

in the cool morning

Season word: aki zakura (*lit*., 'autumn cherry blossoms'

refers to cosmos; mid-autumn)

Mehmet Tuna Uysal

さらさらと

　　風吹く夜の

　　　　竹の春

さらさらと

　　かぜふくよるの

　　　　たけのはる

季語　竹の春（仲秋）

「竹の春」は、たけのこの出る時期、栄養を奪われて衰え
た竹が、秋になると勢いを取り戻し、葉も青々としてくる状
態をさす。

李一一（リー・イーイー、リリー）

Sara sara to

kaze fuku yoru no

take no haru

The wind rustling

in the cool night

the second spring for bamboo

Season word: take no haru (*lit.*, 'bamboo's spring' refers to

the time for bamboo to rejuvenate; mid-autumn)

Li Yiyi (Lily)

林には

　　蟋蟀と鳥

　　　　聖歌隊

はやしには

　　こおろぎととり

　　　　せいかたい

季語　蟋蟀（こおろぎ、三秋）

マイルズ・ハーン

Hayashi niwa

kōrogi to tori

seika tai

In the woods

crickets and birds

choir

Season word: kōrogi (cricket; all autumn)

Mylz Hahn

砂糖黍

　　生計立てる

　　　　無骨な手

さとうきび

　　せいけいたてる

　　　　ぶこつなて

季語　砂糖黍（さとうきび、仲秋）

この句は、貧困に喘ぐ沖縄県民が、ハワイに移住し、砂糖

黍農園を開拓した史実より連想。

劉凱琳（エデリン・ラウ）

Satō kibi

    seikei tateru

      bukotsu na te

The sugarcane

    the rugged hands

      make a living

Season word: satō kibi (sugarcane; mid-autumn)

This was inspired by the impoverished farmers in Okinawa,
who emigrated to Hawaii and worked on the plantations.
Where is their allegiance; Japan or the US?

Edelyn H. Lau

木の下に

　　静かに眠る

　　　　鹿二頭

きのしたに

　　しずかにねむる

　　　　しかにとう

季語　鹿（しか、三秋）

玉真有梨

Ki no shita ni

shizuka ni nemuru

shika ni tō

Underneath the tree

they sleep in tranquility

the two little deer

Season word: *shika* (deer; all autumn)

Yuri Tamama

稲妻や

　　蜻蛉の横を

　　　　突っ走る

いなづまや

　　とんぼのよこを

　　　　つっぱしる

季語　　稲妻（いなづま、三秋）　蜻蛉、とんぼ、三秋）

雷は夏の季語であるが、稲光は、秋の季語となる。

ミーナ・ケセン

Inazuma ya

    tonbo no yoko o

        tsuppashiru

Lightning

    passing right through

        the dragonfly

Season words: inazuma (soft, low lightning; all autumn)

and tonbo (dragonfly; all autumn)

"Inazuma" (soft, low lightning) signifies autumn whereas

"kaminari" (strong lightning) is a season word of summer.

Mina Quesen

降り月

　　過ぎ去りし日々

　　　思い出す

くだりづき

　　すぎさりしひび

　　　おもいだす

季語　降り月（くだりづき、下弦の月、三秋）

「降り月」は、十五夜の満月から下弦の半月へと次第に欠
けていく月のことをさす。

王志茜（山口茜）

Kudari zuki

    sugisarishi hibi

       omoi dasu

The waning moon

    I think of the bygone days

       poignant nostalgia

Season word: kudari zuki (*lit.*, 'descending moon,' but specifically refers to 'waning moon'; all autumn)

Akaneh Wang

秋の雨

　　泣く時笑う

　　　　女の子

あきのあめ

　　なくときわらう

　　　　おんなのこ

季語　秋の雨（あきのあめ、三秋）

ジェミーマ・ウィリアムズ

Aki no ame

   naku toki warau

      on'na no ko

The autumn rain

   when it cries

      the girl laughs

Season word: aki no ame (autumn rain; all autumn)

Jemima Williams

ぴよぴよと

　　妹の手に

　　　　寄る小鳥

ぴよぴよと

　　いもうとのてに

　　　　よることり

季語　小鳥（ことり、仲秋）

メメット・ツナ・ウイサル

Piyo piyo to

    imōto no te ni

        yoru kotori

Tweet tweet—

    a little bird

        cuddled in my sister's hand

Season word: kotori (little bird; **mid-autumn**)

Mehmet Tuna Uysal

October

Photograph 10. "Bamboo Shoot," painting by Shimomura Kanzan (1873–1930), from Sankei Memorial Hall Collection, licensed by Wikimedia Commons, https://commons. wikimedia.org/wiki/ File: Bamboo_Shoot_by_Shimomura_Kanzan,_Sankei_Memori al_Hall.JPG.

旅終えて

　　伝言告げる

　　　　鶫かな

たびおえて

　　でんごんつげる

　　　　つぐみかな

季語　鶫（つぐみ、晩秋）

玉真有梨

Tabi oete

dengon tsugeru

tsugumi kana

Ending the journey

delivering a message

Oh, a dusky thrush

Season word: tsugumi (dusky thrush; late autumn)

Yuri Tamama

一瞬に

　　空飛ぶ秋刀魚

　　　弧を描く

いっしゅんに

　　そらとぶさんま

　　　こをえがく

季語　秋刀魚（さんま、晩秋）

劉凱琳（エデリン・ラウ）

Isshun ni

    sora tobu sanma

        ko o egaku

In a glimpse

    a mackerel pike leaps out of the sea

        making a silver arc

Season word: sanma (mackerel pike, Pacific saury; late autumn)

Edelyn H. Lau

暗い空

　　　冷たい水よ

　　　　　秋時雨

くらいそら

　　　つめたいみずよ

　　　　　あきしぐれ

季語　秋時雨（あきしぐれ、晩秋）

マイルズ・ハーン

Kurai sora

    tsumetai mizu yo

        aki shigure

Dark sky

    the cold water is falling

        autumn shower

Season word: aki shigure (autumn shower; late autumn)

Mylz Hahn

サクサクと

　　踏む葉の夜道

　　　　秋深し

サクサクと

　　ふむはのよみち

　　　　あきふかし

季語　秋深し（あきふかし、晩秋）

李一一（リー・イーイー、リリー）

Saku saku to

    fumu ha no yo michi

        aki fukashi

The crispy sound of fallen leaves

    walking on the road at night

        the deep autumn

Season's word: aki fukashi (deep autumn; late autumn)

Li Yiyi (Lily)

露時雨

　　優しく光る

　　　　森の朝

つゆしぐれ

　　やさしくひかる

　　　　もりのあさ

季語　露時雨（つゆしぐれ、晩秋）

「露時雨」は、露が地面を覆い、雨が降ったように見える光
景のことをさす。

メメット・ツナ・ウイサル

Tsuyu shigure

    yasashiku hikaru

        mori no asa

Countless dewdrops

    shine in the forest

        in the morning light

Season's word: tsuyu shigure (dewdrops that look like

raindrops; late autumn)

Mehmet Tuna Uysal

霧の抱く

　　星無き夜に

　　　　彷徨う子

きりのだく

　　ほしなきよるに

　　　　さまようこ

季語　霧（きり、三秋）

王志茜（山口茜）

Kiri no daku

hoshi naki yoru ni

samayou ko

The fog's sweet embrace

a lone child wandering

in the starless night

Season word: kiri (fog; all autumn)

Akaneh Wang

茸狩や

　　料理する部屋

　　　　良い香り

たけがりや

　　りょうりするへや

　　　　よいかおり

季語　茸狩（たけがり、晩秋）

マイルズ・ハーン

Take gari ya

ryōri suru heya

yoi kaori

Mushroom digging

A cooking room

A subtle scent

Season word: take gari (mushroom digging; late autumn)

Mylz Hahn

刃の如き

　　隙間風吹く

　　　　肌寒し

はのごとき

　　すきまかぜふく

　　　　はだざむし

季語　　肌寒（はだざむ、晩秋）

劉凱琳（エデリン・ラウ）

Ha no gotoki

    sukima kaze fuku

       hadasamu shi

Bladelike wind

    through the window's crack

       cuts through my skin

Season words: hadasamu (skin feeling cold; late autumn)

Edelyn H. Lau

November

Photograph 11. "Crabapple Blossoms in Winter," taken by the editor, November 18, 2019.

初雪や

　　屋根に着く夜

　　　　音もなく

はつゆきや

　　やねにつくよる

　　　　おともなく

季語　初雪（はつゆき、初冬）

劉凱琳（エデリン・ラウ）

Hatsu yuki ya

    yane ni tsuku yoru

        oto mo naku

The first snow

    landing on the roof

        wakes none

Season word: hatsu yuki (first snow of the season; early winter)

Edelyn H. Lau

冬の明星

　　デカルトの

　　　　二元論

ふゆのみょうじょう

　　デカルトの

　　　　にげんろん

季語　冬の明星（ふゆのみょうじょう、三冬）

「明星」は、金星のことを指す。ルネ・デカルト（1596 年–

1650 年）は、フランスの哲学者、数学者。

李一一（リー・イーイー、リリー）

Fuyu no myōjō

Dekaruto no

nigen ron

The Morning Star in winter

a reminder of the dualism

of Descartes

Season word: fuyu no myōjō (Morning Star in winter; all winter)

Morning Star refers to Venus. René Descartes (1596–1650) was a French philosopher and mathematician.

Li Yiyi (Lily)

初氷

　　　お椀の湯気と

　　　　　かつらむき

はつごおり

　　　おわんのゆげと

　　　　　かつらむき

季語　初氷(はつごおり、初冬)

劉小雨(リュウ・シャオユー)

Hatsu gōri

    o wan no yuge to

        katsura muki

The first ice

    the steam of the soup bowl

        and the thin slice of white radish

Season word: hatsu gōri (first ice of the season; early winter)

Liu Xiaoyu

色葉散る

　　君が残した

　　　　紅の跡

いろはちる

　　きみがのこした

　　　　べにのあと

季語　色葉散る（紅葉散る、もみじちる、初冬）

王志茜（山口茜）

Iroha chiru

    kimi ga nokoshita

        beni no ato

The blushing dusk of falling foliage

    what you left behind

        tints my whole world

Season's word: iroha chiru (momiji chiru, falling fall

foliage; early winter)

Akaneh Wang

先のない

　　寂しい道に

　　　　返り花

さきのない

　　さびしいみちに

　　　　かえりばな

季語　返り花(かえりばな、帰り花、初冬)

「返り花」は、初冬の小春日の頃に返り咲く、季節外れの
花のこと。

メメット・ツナ・ウイサル

Saki no nai

samishii michi ni

kaeri bana

The returning blossom

by the lonely road

that leads nowhere

Season word: kareri bana (*lit.*, 'returning blossom' refers

to unseasonal blossoms during winter, after normal

blossoms in spring or summer; early winter)

Mehmet Tuna Uysal

昼下がり

　　温和な気温

　　　　小春日よ

ひるさがり

　　おんわなきおん

　　　　こはるびよ

季語　小春日（こはるび、初冬）

マイルズ・ハーン

Hiru sagari

onwana kion

koharu bi yo

A winter afternoon

a mild temperature

a fine warm day

Season word: koharu bi (warm winter day; early winter)

Mylz Hahn

落ち葉降る

　　栗鼠は驚き

　　　　去ってゆく

おちばふる

　　りすはおどろき

　　　　さっていく

季語　　落ち葉（おちば、三冬）

有梨玉真

Ochiba furu

risu wa odoroki

satte yuku

The dead leaves falling

the startled squirrel

rushes off

Season's word: ochiba (dead leaves; all winter)

Yuri Tamana

学食に

　　　通じる道に

　　　　　　忘れ花

がくしょくに

　　　つうじるみちに

　　　　　　わすればな

季語　忘れ花（わすればな、帰り花、初冬）

「忘れ花」は、初冬の小春日の頃に返り咲く花のこと。

劉凱琳（エデリン・ラウ）

Gakushoku ni

tsūjiru michi ni

wasure bana

On my way to the cafeteria

a forgotten flower

waves goodbye

Season word: wasure bana (*lit.*, 'forgotten blossom' refers

to unseasonal blossoms during winter, after normal

blossoms in spring or summer; early winter)

Edelyn H. Lau

December

Photograph 12. "Red Fox," taken by the editor, June 23, 2020.

夜の空

　　光輝く

　　　　天狼よ

よるのそら

　　ひかりかがやく

　　　　てんろうよ

季語　天狼（てんろう、三冬）

「天狼」は、オリオン座の一等星、シリウスのこと。

マイルズ・ハーン

Yoru no sora

    hikari kagayaku

        Tenrō yo

A night sky

    as bright as can be

        Sirius

Season word: Tenrō (Sirius; all winter)

Tenrō refers to Sirius in the constellation Orion.

Mylz Hahn

日向ぼこ

　　窓の向こうは

　　　　乱反射

ひなたぼこ

　　まどのむこうは

　　　　らんはんしゃ

季語　日向ぼこ（ひなたぼこ、三冬）

劉小雨（リュウ・シャオユー）

Hinata boko

   mado no mukō wa

      ran hansha

Winter sunbathing

   the diffusing reflection of snow

      on the windows

Season word: hinata boko (winter sunbathing; all winter)

Liu Xiaoyu

短日や

　　昼間を無駄に

　　　　ケータイと

みじかびや

　　ひるまをむだに

　　　　ケータイと

季語　短日（みじかび、三冬）

ミーナ・ケセン

231

Mijika bi ya

    hiruma o muda ni

        keitai to

The short winter day

    I waste all my daylight

        lying with my iPhone

Season word: mijika bi (short winder day; all winter)

Mina Quesen

「さようなら」

　　　次会う日まで

　　　　　山眠る

「さようなら」

　　　つぎあうひまで

　　　　　やまねむる

季語　山眠る（やまねむる、三冬）

王志茜（山口茜）

"Sayōnara"

    tsugi au hi made

        yama nemuru

Farewell

    until warmer days I see you again

        the mountains sleep

Season word: yama nemuru (mountains sleep; all winter)

Akaneh Wang

赤狐

　　山の小径と

　　　　絡み合う

あかぎつね

　　やまのこみちと

　　　　からみあう

季語　赤狐（あかぎつね、三冬）

メメット・ツナ・ウイサル

Aka gitsune

yama no komichi to

karami au

The red fox

the mountain trail intertwines

with the fox trail

Season word: aka gitsune (red fox; all winter)

Mehmet Tuna Uysal

フロリダの子

　　霰に驚く

　　　　神の塩かと

フロリダのこ

　　あられにおどろく

　　　　かみのしおかと

季語　霰（あられ、三冬）

ミーナ・ケセン

Furorida no ko

   arare ni odoroku

      kami no shio kato

The girl in Florida

   surprised by the snow pellets

      thinks it is God's salt

Season word: arare (snow pellet; all winter)

Mina Quesen

冬眠や

　　花と動物

　　　　休む時

とうみんや

　　はなとどうぶつ

　　　　やすむとき

季語　冬眠（とうみん、三冬）

マイルズ・ハーン

Tōmin ya

    hana to dōbutsu

        yasumu toki

Hibernation

    animals and flowers

        a season of respite for both

Season word: tōm (hibernation; all winter)

Mylz Hahn

年送る

　　背負った重荷

　　　　置いて行く

としおくる

　　せおったおもに

　　　　おいていく

季語　年送る（としおくる、暮）

劉凱琳（エデリン・ラウ）

Toshi okuru

    seotta omoni

        oite iku

Sending the year off

    leaving behind

        the burden on your shoulders

Season word: toshi okuru (sending off the year; yearend)

Edelyn H. Lau

List of Contributors

Mylz Hahn '23 is a rising senior who is majoring in East Asian Studies with a certificate in Translation and Intercultural Communication. The haiku seminar has been a great experience in branching out into creative writing, especially as a way to practice Japanese in a more artistic way outside of class, as well as being more observant of nature for the ideas that led to the haiku and led to his fall Junior independent writing being a discussion on haiku translation. His dream career is to be a Japanese to English media localizer, combining his passion for Japanese pop-cultural media such as video games and anime, foreign language study, East Asian culture and history, and creative writing.

Udit Basu graduated from Princeton in 2020, with a major in Geosciences (Geophysics) and two minors in Planets and Life, and East Asian Studies (Japanese), where he has conducted extensive research on *hikikomori* (social hermetism of a person who is socially withdrawn and leads a life of abnormal avoidance of social contacts) in Japan. He has been working with Professor Gerta Keller on research relating to the K-T mass extinction (the extinction

of the dinosaurs). He will be going to graduate school to
pursue a Ph.D. to study martian planetary science.

Natalie Diaz graduated from Princeton in 2019, with a
Computer Science major and a certificate in Linguistics.
She currently lives in California, where she works as a
software engineer. She's happy that she can continue
writing haiku, especially during this difficult year.

Edelyn H. Lau '22 is a concentrator in East Asian Studies
with a certificate in Translation and Intercultural
Communication. Growing up in Hong Kong, she was
fascinated by the linguistically diverse materials
surrounding her that she eventually developed a keen
interest in both modern Chinese writing and literature in
translation. Poetry holds a special place in her heart for it
inspires a sensory experience where she is fully captivated
by the imagery, musicality, and sentimentality invoked by
words. In her free time, she likes to experiment in the
kitchen and listen to podcasts. If the weather allows, she
also takes pleasure in ambling through the verdure and
checking out blossoms hidden here and there.

Li Yiyi (Lily) is a graduate student, pursuing a Ph.D. in the Department of Electrical Engineering and Computer Science. Aside from her interest in scientific research, she has a strong passion for Japanese language and culture. Being a heavy watcher of Japanese television, she taught herself Japanese and the basics of haiku poetry. In the process of learning the Japanese language, she developed an interest in translation. Aiming for translating serious literature someday, she is currently an amateur member of a Japanese television shows translation team.

Liu Xiaoyu is a graduating Ph.D. student from the Department of Chemical and Biological Engineering. He becomes interested in haiku after watching the television variety show, "Purebato" (which stands for 'Pressure Battle'). He hopes to capture life experience through writing good haikus. He is excited about sharing his haiku with readers.

Mina Quesen '23 is an English major with a love of all creative arts. She grew up with Japanese and Latinx cultures in her home. Through haiku, she is able to combine her mixed heritage and love of words while also discovering the beauty in everyday nature. Along with being a Mellon Mays fellow and Peer Academic Advisor for Forbes College, she is an Editor-in-Chief of the Nassau Weekly and the Editor-in-Chief Emeritus of Arch & Arrow Literary Collective. Between these publications, Mina has published fiction, poetry, and personal reflections. In her free time, she can be found experimenting with a new recipe or curled up with her latest fiction pick.

Shantanu Ramji '23 is a rising senior with a broad interest in the arts that extends from reading and writing literature to experimenting with visual media. He is a declared Comparative Literature concentrator, with a planned certificate in Creative Writing. Having previously obtained a proficiency in Spanish and German, he discovered a newfound love for Japanese language and culture when he entered the Japanese language program at Princeton, which he plans to continue with to the end of his Princeton career. In addition to his foreign-language poetry, he has written and illustrated cartoons for the Daily Princetonian, hand-illustrated and designed the poster for Princeton in Ishikawa 2021, and contributed articles to Princeton's newly created music blog, For the Record. In his free time, he consumes and creates as much media as physically possible, be it music, anime, manga, books, or drawings.

Lucas Stewart '22 is a senior with a love of knowledge in all its forms. He is majoring in Computer Science, BSE with a certificate in East Asian Studies. Never having taken Japanese before attending Princeton, his love of the language and culture has blossomed over these past four years. He is also a member of Princeton Christian Fellowship and can often be found with his best friends chatting and enjoying life together. When not with friends, he enjoys a good movie on a dark rainy night or reading on his Kindle outside with the warm spring sun above.

Yuri Tamama '22 is a recent graduate of Princeton's Department of Geosciences. An aspiring seismologist, Yuri will pursue a Ph.D. through Caltech's Geophysics program beginning Fall 2022. In her spare time, Yuri enjoys cooking, playing video games, and writing poetry. Her enjoyment of poetry flourished as she engaged in Creative Writing poetry classes and Princeton's haiku sessions.

Mehmet Tuna Uysal is a is a third-year graduate student in the Department of Electrical and Computer Engineering (ECE) studying interacting atomic systems in crystal hosts, while his undergraduate thesis investigated the

optomechanics of helium droplets. He finds that through
these seemingly disjoint subjects, which scale from the
microscopic to the macroscopic, he grew in appreciation of
physical principles that ground our understanding of both
realms. For research and haiku alike, he is motivated by
relations, whether of nature or the individual, that are
simple and beautiful. In his free time, you might find him
reading in the library, running by the stadium or social
dancing in a post-pandemic campus.

Akaneh Wang '24 is a sophomore from New York City
planning to major in civil and environmental engineering.
At Princeton, she is a member of The Prince, Asian
American Students Association, and the Forbes College
Council. In her free time, you can find Akaneh doodling
on a piece of scrap paper or taking a walk in the nearest
park.

Jemima Williams '23 is a rising senior, concentrating on
Politics. She is also involved in French Studies and loves
writing poems in French, English, and Japanese. During
the Covid-19 outbreak, she stayed at her home in London,
England, but returned to Princeton in January 2021.

Mayumi Itoh, editor, is a former Professor of Political Science at the University of Nevada, Las Vegas. She has previously taught at Princeton University and Queens College, City University of New York. In addition to a dozen books about foreign policy and politics, such as *Globalization of Japan* and *The Origins of Contemporary Sino-Japanese Relations*, she has written 30 original haiku anthologies, including *Haikus of All Seasons, Haikus for Hiroshige's One Hundred Famous Scenes of Edo, Haikus for Bashō's Narrow Road to The Deep North, Haikus Inspired by Yoshida Kenkō's Idle Essays, Haikus Inspired by Kamo no Chōmei's Journal of a 100-square-foot Hut,* and *Haikus Inspired by Sei shōnagon's The Pillow Book.*